THE ESOTERIC
TEACHINGS OF
THE GNOSTICS

THE ESOTERIC TEACHINGS OF THE GNOSTICS

by

FRANCES SWINEY

Author of *The Awakening of Women,*
The Cosmic Procession, and
The Bar of Isis.

www.whitecrowbooks.com

The Esoteric Teachings of the Gnostics

Original Copyright © 1909 by Frances Swiney. All rights reserved.
This Copyright © 2015 by White Crow Books

Published and printed in the United States of America and the United Kingdom
by White Crow Books; an imprint of White Crow Productions Ltd.

For information, contact White Crow Books
at 3 Hova Villas, Hove, BN3 3DH United Kingdom,
or e-mail to info@whitecrowbooks.com.

Cover Designed by Butterflyeffect
Interior design by Velin@Perseus-Design.com

Paperback ISBN 978-1-910121-74-0
eBook   ISBN 978-1-910121-75-7

Non Fiction / Religion / Gnosticism

www.whitecrowbooks.com

CONTENTS

FOREWORD

THE four illustrations given in this work are spirit drawings, and were done in the early part of the year 1908 by a woman under spirit control. This lady had no knowledge of colour-symbology, nor did she understand the esoteric meaning of the pictures drawn until in automatic writing the explanation was partly given.

So wonderfully and accurately descriptive did these drawings appear of the text of this treatise, that, at the earnest request of many hearers of my lecture thereon, and through the generous aid of two earnest women sympathisers, they are here reproduced, being somewhat smaller than the originals.

The spirit control always emphasised the truth that in the higher spiritual spheres there are no "faces," only "Light and Colour," but that in teaching mortals in "the World of Form," objective definition is requisite to impress the lesson on the mind.

"The veil is gradually being uplifted dividing mankind from "the invisible helpers" in the Great Unseen. They, knowing the Truth, are ready to impart it to those whose hearts are purified, whose understanding is not darkened, and in whom the Christos, the Divine Life, has quickened. "And then shall my Son be declared, whom thou sawest as a man ascending... And this my Son shall rebuke the wicked inventions of those nations which for their wicked life are fallen into the tempest, and shall lay before them their evil thoughts, and the torments wherewith they shall begin to be tormented, which are like unto a flame, and he shall destroy them without labour by the law which is like unto fire... Then shall they be known who are my chosen, and they shall be tried as the gold in the fire."

—2 *ESDRAS XIII. 32, 37, 38: XVI. 73.*

PREFACE

THROUGHOUT the ages, there have always been minds that have grasped, in some measure, the eternal verities; they have, as it were, caught a transient vision of the whole in all its glory and divinity, and have been surcharged with the Wisdom of the Highest. But the majority of the race have lagged far behind; the general development of the spiritual consciousness in mankind being as gradual as has been the organic evolution. And thus religious beliefs mark the state of consciousness to which human psychology has attained. We now smile at the coats of skin and too solid flesh with which primitive man in his grossness clothed the most sublime ideals of his race. But, even allowing that, the transcendent reality was soon submerged under the materialised form through whose medium it was presented to the world. The divine intuition, like a golden thread of truth, glistens through all the various faiths. Interwoven, in spite of man's incertitude, with the objective manifestations and symbolism was the subjective indivisible entity of everlasting Wisdom.

Forms of belief are but the transitory phases of the Soul in its upward path from consciousness to consciousness, from truth to truth, from revelation to revelation, from glory to glory, until it attains the Light of lights.

But mankind is loath to recognise the ephemeral character of the distinctive creeds that smother the intrinsic verity under external ceremonial, ritual, dogma, theories, codes, canons, conventions, precedents and definitions, until the outward shell imprisons the living truth in an atrophied contraction. We forget that these evolutionary expositions of faith are but resting places for the human soul in its sore travail for self-completion, as it emerges from the material depths. Instead of being rock-bound sepulchres, in which we bury our Christs, or marble fanes, crumbling before the onslaught of Time, they are only tents that are struck in the dawning, when yet another night of darkness has passed away of the ignorance, fatuity and misery of humanity.

We toil during the night, as did the disciples on the Galilean Sea. We behold but the unfathomable blackness of the waters, and the inscrutable vault of the midnight sky. Around us lie obscurity, mystery, and the dreaded Unknown. Yet, when the morn breaks, comes also the sublime revelation. For encircling us are the everlasting bills, and the Christos awaits us on the shore—the shore of a sunlit sea.

ARGUMENT

At Last

I sought Thee, Love, in storm and sunshine,
In Spring and Summer, in the winter's blast,
For, Love, I know Thee, and in Thy Presence
All things change, Thy spells once o'er them cast.

I found Thee, Love, and for a moment
Darkness and light, the earth and sky and sea
Were as naught, for Thou, Love, filled them,
Thou wert in Thy Beauty all Infinity.

I lost Thee, Love, and wept, bereft, forsaken;
I felt the darkness fall on the barren land:
Faintly a star shone; lo! In highest Heaven
Thou—yet Twas I, Love—before God's Throne
didst stand.

"The Woman Soul leadeth us ever upward and on."

Goethe.

THE ESOTERIC TEACHINGS
OF THE GNOSTICS

I T is said by the occultists that the present spiritual evolution - of
man will proceed, not through a new inspiration or a new gospel, but
by a more thorough knowledge, understanding and interpretation
of the ancient and forgotten wisdom of past ages, uniting it in harmony
with the scientific truths gained by modern research. This renaissance
of the religious literature of archaic faiths will come as a revelation to
all who are moved by the spirit to discern the deep esoteric realities underlying the symbolism and phraseology of the seers and mystics of old
times. The modern nations have up to now been fed spiritually upon the
milk for babes; the sublimist truths have been hid from their eyes; they
have been as children, knowing little, but guessing much. Full of hopes
and fears, of surmises, theories, make-believes and illusions.

Possibly, as Mead remarks[1] in Alexandria, in the first century A.D.
the Wisdom-lovers, the various sects of Gnostics, tried to discover a

---

[1] See *Fragments of a Faith Forgotten*.

world-religion, to create a theosophy which would appeal to all minds; but the new race, then springing up, was incapable of comprehending the abstract principles, the abstruse reasoning, the sublime idealisation of the matured Eastern mind; matured by centuries of experience, by aeons of suffering, learning and contemplation. The European peoples, composed mostly of strong, virile barbarians, could not comprehend the subtle arguments, the fine distinctions of the Eastern philosophers. They lost touch with the pristine truths of the higher soul-life, because their consciousness was not sufficiently evolved so as to be able to seize their significance and importance. Like children they put by for a more convenient season the problems of life, which ever demand a solution.

Thus the Gnostics invariably taught the doctrine of reincarnation; they insisted upon the Karmic Law, the inexorable working out of cause and effect; they taught that the Kingdom of Heaven is to be sought for within a man, it is the "blessed nature of all things, which were and are still to be.[2] That the real human is male-female, devoid of differentiated sexuality; the duality of manifestation now existing being a transitory phase of experience; therefore whoever would progress must strive to abandon the dual nature and return to the oneness of the eternal essence, where there is neither male nor female, as now, but a new and complete creature, " the woman perfected," the super-man who comprises and surmounts man.

They believed in the Forgiveness of Sins, but in no vicarious sacrifice for sin. That monstrous doctrine was formulated by men who shrank

---

[2] *Fragments of a Faith Forgotten*, Mead, p. 201.

from living Christ in themselves.[3] Though Gnosticism long preced-
ed Christianity, the Gnostics were the first Christians; they accepted
Christ in the full realisation of the word; his life, not his death, was
the key-note of their doctrine and their practice. Thousands of years
before the Egyptian Seers prognosticated the spiritual evolution of the
soul in the seven stages of probation, in the life beyond the grave. They
conceived of a mystical Christos, a divine type of character that could
only be attained through the soul's conflict with evil in the spiritual
spheres of nebulous idealism. The Gnostics welded the ancient mythos
into mundane practicability. They recognised the divine nature of the
Universe, the eternal progression of all things, and of the human in particular. Therefore, it is easily conceivable that they were misunderstood,
maligned and discredited by the crude primitive minds of the Goth,
the Vandal and the Hun, who had drunk too deeply of the draught, of
oblivion to remember their former phases of existence. The Gnostics
cast their pearls before swine, who straightway turned and rent them.

"The greatest sin of the Gnostics was," says Mead, " that they were
centuries before their time;" for " the Gnostic genius, like a mighty eagle, left the world behind it, and soared in wider and ever wider circles
towards the pure light, towards pure knowledge, in which it lost itself
in ecstasy." But the world-race was not yet ready to receive a full revelation of that highly evolved soul-wisdom. It required a simpler faith
adapted to its needs; the higher mysteries had perforce to be withheld

---

[3] As Jacob Boehme points out, "God in Man gives that which is sinful away. Nobody
can forgive sins except Christ in Man. Whenever Christ lives in Man there is the
absolution."

from the majority of the early Christians, for they laughed them to scorn, or hated what they could not understand, as ignorance has ever done. Thus, by the uninformed, narrow-minded fathers of the primitive Church, the Gnostic heresy or philosophy was suppressed, its followers unrelentingly persecuted and its literature destroyed.

It may truly be said "that the bloodiest and blackest records that history can show us" are the attacks of the Orthodox Church upon the Gnostic mystics, the guardians of the most sacred truths of existence, and the teachers of the higher life of the soul. For we must remember that the normal undeveloped man weighs and judges by his senses, by the things he feels: the reflex action of environment governs and controls his consciousness. For environment is moulding him, not he environment.

We may call it material consciousness of the things seen, the response of the denser grades of matter to outside excitation, the call of life from without in the lower scale of cosmic vibrations as regards their relation to the simpler and obvious phenomena of nature.

But as man develops through sense-experience to the higher consciousness of things unseen, he approximately makes his environment, for knowledge brings relative conquest over conditions. Beyond is wisdom, i.e., harmony with the Universal Consciousness, wherein the unit is perfected. Hence the Gnostics, as the fast decreasing exponents of the old-world knowledge, were imbued with the imperishable memories of the past; from the things seen, felt, and handled they drew the analogy of the things that are invisible, and discovered, to a certain degree, the underlying unity in the Cosmic Procession, through the various stages of manifestation and transmutation.

Gnosticism therefore aimed at the unity of religions, the unity of men in the supreme abstract principles of justice, truth, purity and love, in a universal harmony between the faith and the works; and this at a time when the most irreconcilable theories were in vogue, and men, restless and unsatisfied, hated each other for the love of their Gods. No wonder then that the Gnostics were regarded with suspicion as dreamers of idle dreams, as madmen whose ravings would disturb the smug hypocrisy of the irreligious world, devoted to the letter and not to the spirit; and whose logical reasoning would question the arbitrary dicta of the so-called orthodox Hierarchy which anathematised all orthodoxies but its own. Let them be suppressed. They were an incongrous element in a Church pledged to self-advancement and material gain, whose adherents fought among themselves for supremacy, who should be the greatest. For a man, whether Christian or otherwise, must have his passions, his natural desires, his love of wealth, conquest and power. And thus, for close upon two thousand years, the Gnostics have been under a ban, and their voices silenced.[4] But now another day has dawned.

A day that heralds a clearer, purer light, a day which has sent its rays farther and wider than any day before, and has brought before our eyes much of the ancient wisdom, and many of the long-forgotten gospels of these despised Gnostic philosophers, possibly the greatest mystics

---

[4] "I have repeated whatever may rebound to the glory, and suppressed all that could tend to the disgrace of our religion," wrote Eusebius, that most unscrupulous and arbitrary of expungists and annotators.

11

who ever lived, and also the men who saw deepest into the truth of things. They spoke of that which they knew, of spiritual experience in sublime realities.

In the century before Christ, and in the first and second centuries A.D., there was a strange resemblance to the temper of the last three centuries of our own time. Religion of form and dogma had lost its hold on the educated and the thinkers; "skepticism" and "science" and "misunderstood Aristotelian philosophy were alone worthy the man of genius." There were "emancipated women" also, early pioneers of the liberation movement of their sex; "dialectical daughters," questioning the truth and authority of received opinions; earnest intellectual women, who, joining the leading schools of thought, devoted themselves to the numerous mystic communities established in various parts of the Mediterranean shores; and who, under a perpetual vow of virginity, gave themselves up of their own free will, to the exclusive study of Wisdom's laws. Their longing was not for mortal children, after the flesh, but for a deathless offspring, " which the soul which is in love with the Divine can alone bring forth," not in time but in eternity, born of immortal mind. These spiritual children are now being reborn into the world of manifestation.

Now it is well known that the earliest casuistical writings can only be traced to the second century AD., while the Pauline epistles were never spoken of as sacred inspired Scriptures before A.D. 138, but the earliest prescribed Gnostic gospels can be identified with writers who lived in the latter part of the first century and in the beginning of the second A.D. 'We, therefore, have, in the few mutilated relics that remain of these writings, the most valuable evidence of what primitive Christianity really was, and what was the contemporary opinion of Christ and His teaching. Of these fragments the Coptic translation from the Greek of the Gospel of Pistis Sophia,[5] or the "Faithful Wisdom," is the most remarkable and the most full of valuable instruction to us in these days of dense materialism.

For the theme of Pistis Sophia is the history of the Soul's descent into the grosser forms of matter, and its redemption through the Christos, the Divine Life. Christ, the Risen Lord, Himself relates this cosmic allegory to His disciples for according to the Gnostics, Jesus remained eleven years on earth after the Resurrection, instructing His disciples and the faithful hand of women in many of the mysteries of the 'Kingdom of Heaven, and revealing to them the sublimest truths as they were able to bear them. And many they understood not, for their spiritual eyes had not been fully opened, therefore they erred in the interpretation of the mysteries. Moreover, philosophies, theories, hypotheses, tradition and prejudice had darkened and overlaid the supreme truth of monism, the oneness of cause and effect, of spirit and matter.

---

[5] The only known manuscript was bought by the British Museum, and is catalogued as MS. Add. 5114. There are many fragments from the Books of the Saviour inserted in the MS., which make it of the greater value. See the translation of "Pistis Sophia" by G. R. S. Mead.

PLATE 1

"These drawings are through the Spirit of the maternal Element of the Universe, the Mother the Producer, and the Mother of all who have life. She is the Creatrix, the Father and Mother in one, creating, procreating, giving life, and sustaining life and life itself. The great Father and Mother in one".

In these words this symbolic apotheosis of the Supreme Feminine Principle is described in automatic writing by the Mother of the lady who under spirit control, drew the picture. It is impossible to reproduce the marvellous purity and brilliancy of the colours used, nor to give the brush work in all its delicacy, intricacy, and power.

First, the symbology of colour must be explained. Blue denotes love; yellow, wisdom; carmine, energy. We have, therefore, here depicted Divine love, Divine Omniscience, and Divine Omnipotence, the Divine Trinity in Unity. Yet is love the Supernal from whom power and wisdom precede.

Second, the form is emblematical of Cosmic Processes. The Creative Feminine Principle, as the Eternal Mother, is portrayed emanating whirling clouds and shafts of Divine Energy and Wisdom, surrounded by an atmosphere of Love, in which radiate the white rays of Holiness and the Cosmic Cross of Glory. The head is crowned with the Crown of Dominion, formed of the Seven Virtues or Seven Attributes of the Holy Spirit. The Crown turreted signifying the self-existent and self-creative Power of Divinity. The Divine Mother is thus shown in the Power of Her Love creating the Universe in Wisdom. The Universe is therefore formed by Love, vilified with Energy, and sent in Wisdom.

Men had to a great extent travelled far from first principles and single purposes. They had lost in the maze of their own imagination the golden thread of continuity in the Eternal Procession. First, therefore, Christ emphasised the mystery of the Divine Feminine, "the mystery within the veil," which is before all mysteries, "even the Father in the likeness of a Dove," the Eternal Mother. For in the apotheosis of the masculine phase of soul-consciousness the fundamental truth of the Divine Motherhood was almost obliterated from the existing cults. The exaltation of the Father and the God had infringed on the supreme prerogatives of the Mother and the Creatrix, the self-existent one. The Dove was in all archaic faiths the symbol of the Immaculate Virgin, who of Herself, produced the male, the Father, the Son and the God. The Oneness of the sublime cause was in danger of being forgotten, also the supreme truth that the "Father" shall also attain to the likeness of "the Mother," the supernal Ogdoad, the Maker of Heaven and Earth, of the Upper and Lower Kingdoms. "I am come" says the Christ, "from that first mystery, which is also the last mystery;" and he goes on to explain that all emanations are from that mystery of the Divine Mother, and must return to it, because of it all mysteries exist, and all their regions, or phases of consciousness, for it is their life and substance. Even as science reveals that all life has a feminine origin. By mystery is meant the hidden meaning, the substance and the truth of things manifest; the reality of things unseen, that are only revealed to the Spirit in Man. For matter in all forms is the objective manifestation of Spirit, both being One.

Therefore say the blessed ones who have already entered the light to the soul still struggling on the heavenward way. "Come unto us, for we are thy fellow-members. We are all one and the same, and thou art one and the same. Now, therefore, we have sent thee thy vesture, which indeed is thine from the beginning, which thou didst leave in the last limit, which also is the last mystery of the interior, until its time should he fulfilled. According to the commandment of the first mystery,"[1] i.e., of the Divine Mother, with whom is the arbitration of all things, for being the Creatrix, with Her is the decision of the things that are made.

And the three vestures with which the soul is clothed are Power. Glory and Light; and the greatest is the vesture of Light, for then all things are revealed in truth, and the soul knows all even as it is known. Against this Light and knowledge the powers of darkness, led by Adamus the great tyrant, the lower self, contend. And Christ took from them a third of their power, by his manifestation of the Divine Feminine in the masculine form, and his conquest over evil, decay and death in his own body.

And it is related that Mary, "the most blessed and spiritual one," the intuitive soul of woman—the soul that remembers and understands—gazed as one inspired as she heard the words of the Saviour, and she said unto Him, "Master, give commandment unto me to speak freely," and Jesus, the compassionate, answered and said unto Mary, "Speak freely, Mary, thou blessed one, whom I will perfect in all the mysteries of the dwellers on high, thou whose heart is right for the kingdom

---

[1] "Pistis Sophia." P. 20.

of the heavens more than thy brethren."[2] For intuition is of the Spirit, and needs not to argue and reason, because it perceives and knows the truth. And thus illumination of the mind is by the light of the Christos, the eternal truth itself developing in the soul. Moreover, to the soul that knows, nothing is impossible, it is only the finite that measures the infinite. Mary then shows how the prophet Isaiah - foretold long before how Christ would overcome the rulers of darkness, and the ordainers of the hour. "For in their hands is time not eternity, and they know but the limit of space, not its infinity." And Christ thus commends Mary: "Well said. Mary, since thou art blessed before all women who are on the earth, for thou shalt be the fulness (pleroma) of all fulness, and the perfection of all perfections; and all things thou seekest I will reveal unto thee." For it is the Daughter who alone enters into Zion; the Soul being feminine, the inner then will be as the outer, both alike.[3]

The allegory of "Pistis Sophia" may be taken as (1), the representation of the cosmic Soul in the aggregate, the Divine Feminine Principle of Life working through all grades of matter and consciousness; and (2), the history of each monad or disintegrated part of the universal Spirit of Life, the Eternal Mother, from the Human to the Divine through every stage of self-development. For the Gnostics kept true to the original pristine faith in the Femininity of the Holy Spirit. A truth universally

---

[2] See Ibid. 25.

[3] Now is the probation of the Son, the Man of Sorrows, acquainted with grief. Having no beauty to be desired, we await the manifestation of the Daughter of Peace, beauty and gladness, when "the Kingdom shall come to the daughter of Jerusalem." —Ml. iii. 8.

suppressed in the fourth century A.D., by the male priesthood of the Christian Church. It is from this blasphemy against the Holy of Holies that Christianity has always suffered, and will suffer until the truth is understood and taught.

Christ proceeds to give the revelation of the Soul's descent from the highest sphere of heaven under the symbology of a descent through different aeons or regions of probation wherein the soul encounters in turn a fresh power and ruler. That is to say, in the cosmic procession through every phase of consciousness there are new experiences to be gained, and more complex conditions to be met; more temptations to be overcome; more negations and illusions to be dispelled by Light and Truth.

The triple powers of evil with which the soul in its pilgrimage has to contend are Arrogant, the Love of Dominion; Adamus, the Love of Self, or the lower nature; and the lion-faced Power, the Love of Lust, which is described as the strongest and most evil of all emanations. And these powers grievously assail the virgin soul, when she descends into the thirteenth aeon, the sphere of the mystery of generation. "For," says the ancient Wisdom, "the corruption of man is the beginning of generation;" the degradation of the dual manifestation of the force of Creation in the virgin soul is the original fall. Christ describes how this sphere of dualities is of necessity, but how it grieves the pure soul to pass through it, as it loses the sense of oneness and has in dispersion failed to attain to unity. And he relates how he found the soul, Pistis Sophia, mourning and grieving; for, in gazing into the height she had seen the light of the treasure of light and had assayed to go towards it, and had ceased to perform the mystery of the thirteenth aeon, which is the mystery of generation (that is of diremption or separation) thereupon Arrogant (the love of sex-dominion) and his followers had grievously tormented her. And all the rulers of the twelve aeons or elementary phases of self-consciousness hated her, for she had desired to go into the heights, above them all, and to enter the Light of Lights before her mystery or her probation had been accomplished. But she was still clothed with the Love and the Light and the Purity of the first mystery, the Divine Mother, and it was in vain that the powers of evil strove to take her light from her.

Then Arrogant (the disobedient and rebellious one) emanated from himself the great lion-faced power of Lust, and a host of other material emanations whom he sent down into the lower regions to lie in wait for Pistis Sophia. And they were to take her light and her power from her, because she had thought to go to the height which is above them all; because she had ceased to do their mystery (for the soul ever longs after its lost chastity) and continued to lament, seeking the light which she had seen; as the soul ever remembers its former state, being a germ of the essence of purity. Then, after pursuing and persecuting Pistis Sophia, " Arrogant caused her to gaze into the lower parts, in order that she might there see his light-power which hath the face of a lion (*counterfeiting strength and rigour*), and that she might long after it, that she might betake herself to that region of chaos, and that it might take from her the light which was in her."

"It came to pass, therefore, after these things that she gazed below; she saw the light-power of Arrogant in the lower parts, and she knew not that it belonged to this triple power Arrogant, but thought that it came from the light which she had seen from the beginning in the height . . . and she thought to herself, "I will go into that region to take the light, which the aeons of light have produced for me, so that I may go to the light of lights which is in the height of heights."[4] And she fell into chaos (i.e., into the purgation of matter, without form and void, being uncontrolled by the will); and the lion-faced power Lust and material desire devoured all the light powers that were in Sophia, expelled her light and cast her substance into the off-scourings of matter, where it became fire (the satiety which burns up desire) and darkness (for light becomes darkness and great is that darkness). For the light, by which the lion-faced power of lust beguiled Pistis Sophia was the false astral light of sensual love, emanating from the lower grades of materialised desires. It absorbs all the spiritual light, the divine love of the soul, and depriving it of all power, renders it a prey to every evil influence of lust and passion and illusion. This is the "First Great Lapse" of the Soul from the upward way.

Then is recounted how the soul sang unto the Light, the thirteen songs of her repentance, saying, "O light of lights, in whom I have trusted from the beginning hearken now therefore, O light, unto my repentance. I have gazed into the height that the light in which I had trusted might help me; I saw all the rulers of the aeons in great number angered against me, rejoicing over me, although I had done them no ill; and they hated me

---

[4] "Pistis Sophie", p. 46.

without cause. They have held me in derision. Now, therefore, O light of truth, thou knowest that I have done these things in my foolishness believing that this lion-faced power (*the false love*) belonged unto thee; and because of thy light, I am a stranger to my brethren, the invisibles (the angelic Host) and also to the great emanations of Barbelo (*the virginal Spirit of the first mystery, i.e., the Supernal Mother*). These things have befallen me because I have ardently longed for thy dwelling, and I am in this region grieving, seeking after the light, which I saw in the height o light of lights, I am oppressed with the darkness of this chaos; save me from the matter of this darkness. Let not this darkness cover me, and this lion-faced power of lust, suffer it not to devour the whole of my power entirely; and let not chaos hide my power."

Violence, self-interest, self-assertion, and love of possession were the most baneful manifestations of the Soul's fall into lust, giving rise to fear, distrust, hatred and aggression. And as the soul makes the body, man's material desires brought evil and sorrow, pride ruled his will.

In the second repentance occurs a remarkable sentence, the plaint of womanhood throughout generations. For the soul is the feminine creative principle in man; the inner Being of the Buddhist; the true self of the Brahmins; the pure law of the Zoroastrian,[5] the Christian's in-dwelling Spirit of God.

---

[5] The beauteous maiden who meets the man as he passes the threshold of death, and he recognises as his inner self. "Only," says Paracelsus, "when man realises the presence of God in him will he begin his infinite life, and step from the realm of evanescent illusion into that of permanent truth." He then knows that he is the "Heavenly and indestructible offspring of a Divine and Incorporeal nature."

The Feminine is therefore the inner nature of man, and woman as the most highly evolved organism and the repository of the creative forces, is the objective representative of the Divine Feminine. The spiritual feminisation of the race proceeds as woman, more and more, frees herself from the gross bonds of differentiated sexuality. This supreme truth is duly emphasised in this allegory. It is remarkable to note through history how at certain epochs, when the civilisations painfully built up by men touched their zenith, their rapid decline followed through the degradation and sex-subjection of women, unjustly discriminated against by law, custom, prejudice and religion. Women, the higher self, was both feared and distrusted by the lower self, man, who, through his increasing materialism, became physically the stronger, and thus subjected the more spiritual factor to his rule and abuse. Consequently mankind ceased to advance, while the steady deterioration of the mothers of the race thus prejudicially affected was the inevitable result, the inexorable karma of deeds done in the flesh. "Disease and sorrow and mortification are the fruits which the tree of the mortal's own demerits bears."[6]

Thereupon "Pistis Sophia", the faithful Wisdom, cried and said, "Now, therefore, O light, leave me not in chaos until the end of all my time. They sought to take away the whole of my light to the very exterior; (i.e., the body becoming more and more defiled, corrupt, and diseased), they have set a watch on my power; saying one to another together—for my light had abandoned me—Seize her, take from her

---

[6] Hindu saying.

all the light which is in her. Therefore, O light, go not far from me; save me, O light, save me from the hands of these pitiless ones." For the masculine materiality has ever striven to overcome the feminine spirituality. It is ever at war with it, until it understands the unity underlying all things.

What is more, "Man, having become separated from the woman (the soul) in him, lost his true light."[7] and not only quenched the living spirit within him, but degraded to the basest abuse the woman of the race, the objective spiritual power of man. And thus the lust of man dragged down womanhood into the darkness of impurity and all uncleanness, for " men loved darkness rather than light because their deeds were evil."

And when Pistis Sophia had uttered her ninth song of repentance, her repentance was accepted by the first mystery (the Mother of Mercy) and Christ was sent by commandment to help her. And he led her out of chaos in that she had repented and had trusted in the light, the Divine Love; for she had endured these great tribulations and these great perils, because she had only been deceived by a stream of Light, the false love and desire, in that it resembled the light in which she had trusted. But the powers of evil became more and more enraged and cast forth hosts of exceedingly evil emanations when they saw the Christ[8] coming in aid of Pistis Sophia, and they pressed upon her and

---

[7] Paracelsus.

[8] i.e., the higher life evolving in the Soul, and hating the things in which the lower nature delighted.

constrained her sorely, and she cried unto Christ to save her, saying, "They among whom I have been sent, desired to take away my light they loved to descend into the darkness. I could not stand in their midst . . . my matter hath been bound, because of my light which they have taken away." For the lust of the flesh, the lust of the eyes, the pride of life, and the deceitfulness of riches choked the growth of the soul, the woman spirit of intuition became blurred; the spiritual vision darkened, the creative force weakened, the font of life contaminated. In sensuality and the depths of impurity mankind extinguished the inner light of the woman, and bound, in the grossest meshes of the flesh, the soul that would have risen to the light. Even the material substance of woman, the objective manifestation of the subjective soul, has been debased and impregnated with evil, so that the powerful potentialities of her finer physical nature have been rendered all but impotent, being weakened by the admixture of that which was corruptible. Man's nature has to be purified by the exaltation of the objective womanhood and through the development of the subjective woman. Man in the crucible of renunciation frees himself and the woman, and, in the cleansing fire of regeneration, rises above his desire.

Then Christ relates how he emanated from himself a great light-power, and sent it forth to bring Pistis Sophia out of the depths of chaos,[9]

---

[9] The conscious recognition of the individual soul of its own divinity and oneness with the Divine, and this knowledge inspires the courage and fortitude to rise above the world and its delusive snares and pleasures. As Jacob Boehme writes, "He who knows his own divine self knows the whole of the universe." In the Holy Spirit, the Divine Feminine is the root of all life and light.

and Pistis Sophia rose into the heights, and sang a song of praise unto the Light; and when she had uttered her last song of repentance, in that hour was fulfilled the statute of all the tribulations with which Pistis Sophia had been disgracefully inflicted, for the consummation of the first mystery, that is, the Divine Feminine, which is from the beginning; for the time had come to rescue her from chaos and lead her out of all the darkness, for her repentance had been accepted by the Mother of Life, to wit, the soul's consciousness had evolved to know the evil and the good, and to choose the good for evermore.

And it came to pass, therefore, when the light stream of the Christos, the Divine Life, had infused into Pistis Sophia all her light powers (the soul's latent-potentialities), which had been taken from her by the emanations of Arrogant and the lion-faced power of lust, that she became entirely radiant; and the other light powers (the inherent and intrinsic spirituality) which Arrogant could not take away from Pistis Sophia, regained their brilliancy, and were joyful and full of light. And the great light-stream surrounded Pistis Sophia on every side, on the right hand and on the left, and became a crown of light upon her head, signifying the perfect development of the supreme virtues. And yet again the powers of evil attack and harass Pistis Sophia, changing their shapes, in order to take her light from her, for even when the Soul, "the woman" is free, she will still have to suffer great tribulation on the part of the imperfect male element, the Time-Spirit, the Workman, or, as the Gnostics termed it, "the Deficiency" in the Cosmos. For as the consciousness becomes more developed, so it becomes more sensitive to excitation, and "the dignity and excellence of the human Soul lieth not in her simplicity but in her complexity. She is the summit of evolution, and all generation works in order to produce her," and generation involves disintegration and death, for the transmutation of the material to the spiritual; therefore the great contest of the Soul is with the lower forces of the creative energy as she strives to transcend them to the higher.

But from these fresh persecutions and daemonial powers is Pistis Sophia, rescued by the Archangels Gabriel and Michael, (signifying Strength and Service), who bear her in their hands so that her feet should not touch the lower darkness and be defiled. For the angels Of God (the evolved consciousness of truth, purity and love) encompass the soul who knows them as they are. To that soul evil is no more present but is of the past. She has found " the thing itself which lies behind all appearances," and in herself has developed the creative centre, the balance of forces which can only be in the One. "I live," cries the enlightened soul, " yet not I. but the Christos, the Divine Life."

Then the liberated Soul of Wisdom took courage exceedingly, and she no longer feared the emanations of Arrogant nor his power, nor did she tremble before the daemonial power of Adamus, the lower self. And thus Pistis Sophia was tabernacled in the midst of the light. And all the emanations of Arrogant could no longer change their appearance (for illusions have no being in Truth); nor could they stand the shock of the great light-stream which formed a crown on the head of Sophia (the Woman crowned with the Sun;) and all the emanations of

Arrogant collapsed, because of its mighty radiance, and the shadows of darkness fled, for the 'illuminated soul sees only light in the perfect day, and all invisible things are made plain in the things that are seen. The Powers of Evil could no longer at all draw nigh unto Pistis Sophia, because of the great light, and could do her no harm because she had trusted in the light.

Then Christ relates how by order of his Father the first mystery looking within (that is contained in the Divine Mother) I; the first mystery, looking without (*that is the Son, the Manifestor of the Divine Mother*) also descended into chaos shining most exceedingly. "I directed my attack against that lion-faced power (lust) and took from it all its light; I prevented all the emanations of Arrogant from entering from that hour with their region, which is the thirteenth aeon, (*the aeon of generation; for generation is of necessity, not evil in itself, but in abuse*), I took away the power of all the emanations of Arrogant, and they fell into chaos, powerless. And I led Pistis Sophia forth from chaos, treading under foot the serpent-headed emanation of Arrogant, clothed in the garment of shame, and the seven-headed basilisk emanation, the lion-faced power, and the dragon-faced, and I made Sophia stand upon it. And I, the first mystery (*the Supernal Mother, and, as the Christos, the Son, even the Daughter,*) I took all the powers which were in it, and destroyed all its matter, so that no seed should arise from it from that hour."[10]

Herein the Son becomes pure even as the Father is pure. We must always bear in mind that one truth, one law, permeates all activities.

---

[10] See "Pistis Sophia," p. 138. Words in italics, mine, to elucidate the meaning.

The material individual phases of consciousness are identical with and analogous to the spiritual and cosmic progress.

PLATE 2

"Soul of Bliss and also Adoration in active form intense."

Thus wrote the Controlling Spirit explanatory of this drawing. Herein is depicted a highly evolved soul, replete with Divine Energy, fulfilling the Divine Will in Love and Wisdom. The Soul is clothed with the garments of Righteousness, and is serenely glad in the ecstasy of service in the Highest Good. Evil can nevermore come near this soul, for she is overshadowed by the Holy Spirit of the Divine Feminine. She has past into the Supreme Consciousness of Being, wherein naught but the Beauty of Holiness is conceivable, or ought that offendeth, and in the Pure Light of Truth she knows all truth even as she herself is known. In the aura around the head the Helmet of Salvation is faintly discernible in the mass of potential energy emanating from the soul, for the soul has the saving power of Goodness, and the wings of inherent Might, she can ever perform the Divine Behest. With her is Peace and Joy and Contentment in the Ways of Righteousness. She is entering the Light of Lights, and is becoming Pure Light Herself, as a flaming spirit around the throne of God.

The Christos, the Divine Life, is here identified with the Supernal Mother, the immaculate source of all Life. The Human is united with Divinity, having attained to the full measure and stature of the spiritual powers, the perfected virtues composing the crown of glory.

We must also remember that the Holy Spirit of life is feminine, as shown in its creative energy, being will in action, in motion and generative function. Thus the Christos is the "Son" or manifestation of "the Virgin" and of the Spirit, both being feminine and immaculate. And the "Son" is ever "the Heir," having nothing but what he inherits from the Mother, the Creatrix of Being.

Herein is also certainly portrayed the redemption of the body, the Apotheosis of the perfected human body, glorious in individual completeness. Here is foreshadowed the advent of the virgin birth. The seed of the man shall cease, only the seed of the woman shall endure: for in the perfected being there is no need of change, decay or death, and generation is death. "And he who is born of God keepeth his seed within him." The basilisk-like power, the seven-headed hydra of fallen humanity, is incontinence, the prostitution of the divine creative power to sexual gratification, therefore the children produced by it are children of darkness, not children of the light, of fire and sword and the breaking up of nature's laws; they have been in truth spawn of the devil of lust, begotten and shapen in iniquity, wherewith the whole world has been overspread.[1]

---

[1] "Man's unholy passions have hurried him into an abyss of physical perdition, wherein who has obliterated his "image" and "gifts." *The Rosicrucians: Their rites and mysteries.* Hargrave Jennings. Vol. II., p. 170.

And Pistis Sophia sang another song of praise unto Christ, wherein she says, "Thou hast given me power to unloose the bonds of the emanations of Adamus (*the lower self*) and thou hast smitten the seven-headed basilisk serpent (*the lust forces of generation*), thou hast cast it far from my hands; and thou hast set me above its matter. (*The male element of disintegration and decay*). Thou hast caused it to perish, so that its seed should not arise from this hour forth. And I have become a pure light power.[2] And thus Pistis Sophia became radiant like the invisibles (*the Angels of God*); she renewed her strength like an eagle, and dwelling in the heights she became the same as she was in the beginning (*self-procreative, complete in herself, immaculate*), and no rulers of the aeons could prevail against her; and she rejoiced and was glad, for she knew that the mysteries were given to the race of men, and each Soul shall rest in the aeon of which it has received the mystery of the kingdom of light, and shall come into its inheritance of light. For each soul shall be where the desire of life, of its own individuated consciousness, projects it. Each Soul can only ascend to where its treasure is, where in eternity it has formed its ideal.

Hence we comprehend, as this world is obviously still in the masculine phase of existence, elementary and tentative, why the consciousness of the vast majority of individuals has not yet developed sufficiently to apprehend the Supernal Ideal of the Divine Feminine. Their eyes are holden, and they see diversity where there is but One. Their desire of life is still diffusive instead of concentrated. And consequently, as is

---

[2] "Pistis Sophia". Mead, p. 153.

demonstrated by so many of the so-called communications from the Borderland, souls linger long in the thought spheres in which they have shaped the masculine trinities and dualities, until the higher mystery or consciousness is evolved in them; even the apotheosis of the ever-lasting Father is a phase of the cosmic consciousness or idealisation of thought—projection which each soul must experience as it evolves.

We read that after Christ had related the history of Pistis Sophia the disciples asked him many questions, but Mary, the pure, asked him the most profound and searching, for her mind was ever comprehending the hidden meaning of the allegory. And thereby she drew upon her the displeasure and reproach of the disciples, who jealously regarded her intelligent demeanour. We here have a key to the attitude of Peter and afterwards of Paul towards womanhood as set forth in their epis-tles (and faithfully copied by the Churches in their inversion of sub-lime truths), and we gather that their assumption of male superiority had not the sanction of the Master.

For even in the presence of the Lord, and in this solemn assembly of earnest souls seeking after the light, the arrogance, selfishness and jeal-ousy of masculine sex-bias are evinced in all their inherent meanness, envy and antagonism to sex-equality of opportunity, as the following incidents demonstrate. The Christ asks if his words are understood, and Mary's reply is forestalled by Peter, who, starting forward, said unto Je-sus: "Master, we cannot endure this woman to thus take our place from us, and not suffer us to speak, but she speaks many times." And when Mary would again interpret the mystery of the song of Pistis Sophia she says, "Master my mind is ever comprehending, so that I could come forward every time and expound the interpretation of the words which she spoke, but I fear Peter for he hath threatened me, and hateth our sex." And Christ replies to her. "No one shall prevent whosoever shall be filled with the spirit of light from coming forward and expounding the interpretation of what I say. Now, therefore, O Mary, expound the interpretation of the words uttered by Pistis Sophia."

And Christ ever commends her answers, and says: "In the place where I shall be there will be also my twelve ministers, but Mary Magdalene and John, the virgin, shall be higher than all the disciples."

"We are told in the fragment remaining of the Gospel of Mary, that when the Saviour had departed from the disciples fear and doubt assailed them, and they said, 'How can we go to the heathen and preach the gospel of the kingdom of the Son of Man; if they have not received him, how will they receive us? 'Then Mary arose, and having embraced them all, spake unto her brethren, 'Weep not, and be not sorrowful, nor doubt, for His grace will be with you all and will overshadow you. Let us rather praise His goodness that he hath prepared us, and made us to be men.' Peter requests her to proclaim what the Lord has revealed to her, thus acknowledging the great distinction which the Lord had always permitted her above all women. Thereupon she begins the narrative of an appearance of the Lord in a dream; unfortunately some pages (*of the original MS*) are here missing. Hardly had she finished when Andrew arises and says he cannot believe that the Lord has given such novel teachings. Peter also rejects her testimony and chides her. And Mary in tears says unto him: "Peter, of what dost thou think? Believest thou that I have imagined this only in myself, or lied as unto the Lord?"

And now Levi comes forward to help Mary, and chides Peter as an eternal quarreller. How the dispute went on we cannot determine, as two pages are missing."[3]

But the incident is instructive, and throws a lurid light upon the sinister reason for the wholesale destruction of the Gnostic writings, which so clearly taught the mystery of the oneness of sex, the limitations of the masculine element, as the Workman of Time, decay, and Death, the supremacy of the Divine Feminine, and the absolute necessity of chastity in the path to the Higher Life. When the waters of Jordan flow upward then will be born "the Race of Mind," "the people whom the Lord has made."[4] How was so sublime a doctrine, so practical a religion, so pure an ideal, to find acceptance in an age of sensuality and gross lasciviousness, in an age when the lust of the flesh and the pride of life ruled men's desires, and were the goal of their aspirations?

Testimony is gathering fast round the first century of the Christian era, and many facts tend to show how simple, clear and undogmatical were the teachings of the early followers of the Christ. Christianity consisted in living a life, not expounding a theology. As the

---

[3] See *Fragments of a Faith Forgotten*, Mead, p. 502. It is very suggestive of a sinister motive, that in most of the erasures and where pages are missing in these Gnostic writings, the subject treated of in the context is of some hidden mystery, the interpretation of which was unacceptable to the masculine mind and to bigoted orthodoxy.

[4] "The Lord " Adonai," in the original Hebrew, is the name substituted for the supreme title of the Mother, Jehovah, which, because of its feminine nature, the Jews are forbidden to mention, and give that of "the Son" instead.

life became too hard, too strenuous an effort, too idealistic of realisation, the primitive church more and more whittled away the necessity of practice, and laid greater weight on dogma. They ignored
the Christ's standard or criterion of discipleship. "Whosoever doeth
the will of my Father shall know of the doctrine." Now the will in all
archaic mysteries is Feminine, therefore the will of God is the will
of the Supreme Good, the Mother. It is the Law of the Mother. And
what truth was harder for the sex-biased, prejudiced Jewish people to
embrace than the perfect equality of man and woman, and the spiritual supremacy of the Feminine Spirit in mankind, though taught
externally in their Scriptures, and demonstrated esoterically in their
ritual'? The early Fathers with the Gentile converts therefore subvert-
ed the whole truth into a half-truth, which, as we know, is then a lie.
Instead of regarding woman as the intuitive spiritually susceptible
factor in the race, and therefore the medium for the transmission of
the higher subjective qualities, they anathemised her as a purely sexual adjunct to humanity, and circumscribed purity to the objective
dishonour, and economic, canonical and political disfranchisement
of womanhood. I use the word "dishonour" with intent. To touch a
woman was considered by these saintly hypocrites contamination.
Women were considered unclean and unholy. They were not allowed
to profane the inner sanctuaries of the churches, which often their
munificence and piety had built; their naked hands might not touch
the altar cloths, nor take the sacramental bread. "Woman!" exclaims
Tertullian, "thou art the gate of Hell."

No wonder that these monstrous teachings led to the persecution, degradation and maltreatment of womanhood during those ages well termed "dark," and which, for immorality and sensual debauchery, equalled in the end the excesses of the Roman Empire. For, deprived of her rights, her natural status and prerogatives, woman became chattel, slave and tool for man's use and abuse. Yet the Gnostics had taught that the woman nature is the genuine representative of the purely human out of which evolves the divine. They repudiated the Hebrew tradition which ascribed the origin of evil to woman, but on the contrary declared that woman, longing to he wise, became the recipient of the heavenly Wisdom, being more susceptible to divine influences than man; and that it is through the woman the race had been raised.

They did not discard and ignore the cumulative testimony of the ages, personified in the Female Serpent Deities of the archaic faiths, who symbolised all the divine powers; as, for instance, the Egyptian serpent-headed goddess, Hebe, called "the maker of invisible existences apparent," the revealer of the unseen world. "The chariot of the soul is drawn by mothers," wrote Lamblichus. They direct its course through the lower and upper kingdoms. They take it to the entrance of the light spheres, where the maidens are the keepers of the unveiled light powers of the Soul. The Serpent of Evil, Apophis, is always symbolised as male and an enemy of the Soul. Moreover, as the feminine was the beginning of life in the material world, so, reasoning by analogy, from the natural to the spiritual from things seen and experienced to things invisible, the Gnostics recognised that the Divine Mother was the Source of all in the realms of the Ineffable. She was the great Silence, the state beyond being, containing in itself everything potentially from which the Father and the Son proceed, and she is also the Pleroma, the consummation of all in the supernal unity.

It was, therefore, a hard lesson that Gnosticism set before the human race. The vestures of light with which the human soul in her time of probation was to clothe her nakedness, were the attributes of the Divine Feminine, the seven daughters of eternal Wisdom—"Love, joy, hope, long suffering, gentleness, goodness, faith." Moreover, from the Virgin Spirit, the perfect Power, wherein is the unnamable Father, proceeds Thought, Foreknowledge, Incorruptibility and Life Everlasting, all described as Feminine entities.

Thereupon says the Christ: "Gain for yourselves, ye sons of Adam, by means of these transitory things, which are not yours, that which is your own and passeth not away." These things of the world of sense are fleeting and unsubstantial, but these eternal gifts of the Spirit are the heritage of the race, the true Human born in the likeness of the Divine Mother. Yet, through the consciousness gained in all the lower phases of experience, the soul would gather to itself the finer, purer sensations, and thus weave for herself her garment of light, being clothed with the righteousness of the Christos. It was this esoteric womanhood, this underlying and interior feminity of humanity that Christ disclosed to his disciples, which, evidently, they misunderstood, and garbled with their own erroneous, crude, and gross definitions. He explains how only in the Highest, in the supreme Divine Nature, are the various spheres or aeons free from imperfections that there are states of progression even among the angels that no stage of spiritual development is free from the presence of that mixture, which tends to disintegration, change and mutability, until each on or phase of development has been perfected in the individual monad.[5]

This statement throws a light upon the answer of Christ to the suppliant for eternal life, "Why callest thou me good? There is none good but one; that is God." The word here used in the Hebrew is "the Elohim," the Divine Mother of Life, the Pleroma of perfect fulness of the Gnostics. St. Paul had a premonition of this truth when he said that in the Christos the fulness of the Godhead dwelt, for by inheritance the Divine Life in the monad attains to all things that are contained in the Supernal Mother.

The seeming interminableness of this cosmic process of redemption appalled the disciples. "What soul," they asked, "can be saved?" But Christ demonstrates how little the finite mind can comprehend the things of infinity, for "I say unto you, it (the soul) shall he in all the

---

[5] We must remember that Christ here deals with the Cosmic Procession in the abstract and of the human race in the concrete. Each aeon is at the same time a state, *not* a place, and a place defined by a state. For instance, our solar system is only one phase of progression for the soul, when considered in its relative insignificance with the vast systems of the illimitable Firmament, but each planet is a place of development for the greater and higher phases of consciousness. Probably, in all, there is sex differentiation, our solar system being in the sphere of generation and incompleteness. Yet many mystics affirm that the termination of the male probationary period of this planet is at hand, as the pure womanly aspect of humanity is more and more developed, and "the in-dwelling woman" is revealed in both man and woman. The Soul is potentially complete in herself. She has no need of extraneous entities, her true affinities are her own inherent powers: all else is illusion, and is an emanation from lust in the astral world. Like curses, the Soul's desires return in reflex action and disturb the pure currents of aspiration. The Soul must find her own centre, must be self-poised, nor be dependent on any other entity for development. She must tread the winepress alone; her own arm must bring her Salvation.

regions during the time a man can shoot an arrow." As on the cross he said to the dying thief, "This day shalt thou be with me in Paradise." For the great transmutation of matter will have taken place—in the twinkling of an eye we shall be changed. In each monad are the potentialities of the Whole awaiting development, and the divine touch sets the springs of life in motion. "The light that is not on sea or land," illumines the heart, and immediately it is made whole. And Andrew (*the Materialist*) answered and said: "I am in great wonderment and amazement how many men from this world, and in bodies of matter when they depart from this world, shall pass through all those firmaments, and those rulers, all lords, all gods, all those great invisibles, so that they pass through them and inherit the kingdom of light. This matter, then, is hard for me." When Andrew had said these words the spirit of the Saviour was, moved in him, and he cried out and said: How long shall I bear with you, how long shall I suffer you? Do ye still not know and are ye ignorant? Know ye not, and do ye not understand that ye are all angels, all archangels, gods and lords, all rulers, all the great invisibles, all those of the midst, those of every region of them that are on the right, all the great ones of the emanations of the light with all their glory, that ye are all, of yourselves and in yourselves in turn, from one mass and one matter, and one substance; ye are all from the same mixture.

"And by the commandment of the first mystery (*the Divine Mother*) the mixture is constrained until all the great light-emanations with all their glory are purified until they are cleansed from the mixture, until they are purified, not of themselves, but of necessity, according to the regulation of that one and only ineffable.

"They indeed have not at all (in reality) undergone sufferings, nor changes of region, nor have they torn themselves asunder, nor poured themselves into different bodies, nor have they been in any affliction.

"Whereas ye others, ye are the purgation of the treasure, ye are the purgations of the region of them that are on the right, ye are the purgations of all the invisibles, and of all the rulers; in a word, ye are the purgations of all of them. And ye have been in great afflictions and great tribulation in your pourings into different bodies of this world. And after all these afflictions which came from yourselves, ye have struggled and fought, renouncing the whole world and all the matter that is in it; and ye have not held your hands in the fight, until ye found all the mysteries of the kingdom of light, which have purified you, and transformed you into refined light, most pure, and ye have become pure light itself.

"For which cause have I said unto you aforetime, Seek that ye may find.' I said therefore unto you, 'Ye shall seek out the mysteries of light (*the virtues of the Spirit, truth, love, justice, holiness.*) which purify the body of matter, and they will transform you into light of exceeding great purity.

"Amen, I say unto you, the race of human kind is of matter. I tore myself asunder, I brought unto them (*the knowledge of*) the mysteries of light, to purify them, for they are the purgations of all the matter of their matter: otherwise no soul in the whole human kind could have been saved: nor could it have inherited the kingdom of light, unless I had brought unto them the purifying mysteries.

(The mysteries are within man's own being. Man evolves from within outwards. "Whoso seeketh Wisdom early shall have no great travail: for he shall find her sitting at his door.") For this cause I said unto you aforetime, They that are whole need no physician, but they that are sick; ' that is to say, they that are of the light have no need of the mysteries, for they are pure light-powers, but the human race hath need of them, for (men) are purgations of matter, *(i.e., Man was evolved from the lowest phase of matter, as biology demonstrates)*. For this cause, therefore, preach ye to the whole human race, saying, 'Cease not to seek day and night, until ye have found the purifying mysteries. *(The mystery of healing, of raising from the dead, of regeneration, and of immortality.)* Renounce the whole world and all its associations, that ye may, not add fresh matter to the matter already in you;[6] stay not your hands until ye have found the purifying mysteries which shall cleanse you, and will transform you into pure light, that ye may enter into the height, and inherit the height, and inherit the light of my kingdom.' "

As St. Paul said, "we are the offscourings," and his use of this particular phrase is a proof that he was imbued with the Gnostic teaching

---

[6] Hence the absolute need of chastity and continence, if the soul would attain to the greater mysteries; a truth taught the initiates in every religion. The physical body must be kept pure, and the life forces husbanded in the system for transmutation into the higher elements. But as Jacob Boehme points out, "The mission of woman to save man ceases only when man has found the Celestial Virgin within himself." Woman must still spiritually lead men. "If man were truly to realise his own divine state there is no power that would retain him against his will in his semi-animal body."—Jacob Boehme. And the true woman is the Eternal Virgin.

and doctrine, though he had not understood its mystery. However, much that is ascribed to him are not truly his own opinions, but are interpolations of a much later date, when the Church Fathers assiduously doctored up the fragmentary literature of the early Christians, so as to suit their own convenience, hypotheses and inventions.

Then Christ continues, "Now, therefore, thou, O Andrew, and all thy brethren and co-disciples, because of your renunciations, and all the sufferings ye have endured in every region, because of your repourings into different bodies, and because of your tribulations, ye have, after all, received the purifying mysteries, and are become pure light exceeding refined. For this cause, therefore, ye shall enter into the heights, ye shall come to the interior of all the regions of all these great emanations of the light, ye shall be kings in the kingdom of light forever. And all the regions shall sing a song before you, until ye have entered into the region of the kingdom." For there is joy in the kingdom of heaven over every sinner that repenteth, over every soul that hath attained.

Science daily is stretching forth eager hands into the unknown, and discovering in some measure the mysteries of matter, seen and palpable. In radioactivity we have the transformation and transmutation of elements. We are beginning to discover the laws governing the dematerialisation of matter. We come indeed as near as may be to the life of matter. For there is no such thing as dead matter. Psychology is pressing hard on the heels of the physical. We are learning the law of vibration. We are beginning to have some slight conception of the mechanism of sensation, of the substance of abstract virtues, of the development of the individual consciousness, the Ego's growth from one plane of sensation and experience to another.

PLATE 3

"Soul in deep meditation, wrapped in sublime thought and faith. Calm strength."

In these words the Spirit Control explains this drawing. The symbology both of colour and form is most remarkable, and requires further interpretation. First, there are five colours used: purple and violet, the colour of initiation, is introduced in the aura of the soul, demonstrating that the soul has been initiated into the Divine Mysteries, and has attained unto Love, Power, and Wisdom. She has entered the Holy of Holies through the Door of Divine Intelligence.

Second, the form indicates an indrawing, a conservation of energy. The Soul has retired within herself from active service, for the force emanating from her is potential. She is calmly resting in the Divine Love and the Supreme Wisdom, which completely surround her. But even during contemplative peace, the Love Principle is still active and sends forth rays of Light in the likeness of the wings of a dove, for love seeks not her own, and must ever diffuse her radiance. The soul bears on her head the insignia of her triumphant aeon. She has transmuted matter into spirit, and formed of it the Creative Centre and the Cross of Glory. The Circle and the Cross of her humiliation have become the Circle and the Cross of Divine Motherhood, the Unity of Love, Power, Wisdom, and Beauty. She has entered the Divine Love Principle, therefore, God the Supreme Good abided in her, and within herself she can see God, for the Kingdom of God is within her.

The grossest materialist is fain to confess that heredity does not account for the phenomena of genius; that no theory, on the strictly material plane, can explain the difference between the embryonic mental equipments of the savage and the inborn talents and virtues of the musician, the painter, poet, philanthropist and philosopher. The scientist of the present day is on a level in one respect with the average man in the street, both have lost the old-world knowledge of reincarnation yet in these early Gnostic writings of the first Christians this cosmic truth was fully explained and enunciated by Christ himself. He describes how a sinful soul is brought back time after time to re-birth after it has been brought before the Virgin of light, who will judge it. "And the Virgin of light sealeth that soul, and handeth it over to one of her receivers, and will have it carried into a body, which is the record of the sins which it hath committed."

Here is the law of heredity; as the soul is attracted to those like particles of matter, gross and unrefined, or purified and spiritualised, in which it has passed its last sojourn on earth. The soul reincarnates on its demerits not on its attainments. It has to pay the very last mite. Just as the chemical-physical ingredients of matter are sifted, refined, purified, transformed and transmuted on the material plane in the matrix of the mother, so on the psychic and spiritual plane, all mental qualities and conceptions are brought to the test of the judgment of the Divine Feminine. The Spirit of God judgeth the works whether they be of God. "Amen, I say unto you, she will not suffer that soul to escape from the transmigrations into bodies until it hath given signs of being in its last cycle according to its record of demerit." "Who so committeth sin is the servant of sin. And the servant abideth not in the house forever, but the Son abideth ever. If the Son therefore shall make you free, ye shall be free indeed." That is to say in the occult sense, the soul that sins must return to the probationary stage until it is purged from impurity through the development of the Christos, the Divine Life, that is the same yesterday, today, and forever. The Woman in Man also now rejudges the more inquisitorially, the more uncomprisingly the masculine code of conduct, as the feminine spirit illuminates the heart and the conscience.

Christ further warns the disciples against putting off the redemption of the soul to a more convenient season. The spiritual oil must be bought while the opportunity offers, or the light of the soul flickers out in the darkness. "Strive together," says he, "that ye may receive the mysteries of the light (*i.e., of the higher consciousness*) in this time of stress and enter into the kingdom of light. Put not off from day to day, and from cycle to cycle, in the belief that ye may succeed in obtaining the mysteries when ye return to the world in another cycle; for when the number of perfect souls shall be completed, I will then shut the gates of light, and from that time none will be able to come in thereby, nor will any go forth thereafter, for the number of perfect souls shall be completed and the mystery of the first mystery is completed, before I set fire to the world, that it may purify the whole world, and also all the matters that are still in it, the race of human kind being still upon it. At that time, then, the faith will show itself forth more and more, and also the mysteries in those days. And many souls shall pass through the cycles of transmigration of body, and come back into the world in those days, and among them shall be some who are now alive and hear me teach concerning the consummation of the number of perfect souls, and in those days they shall find the mysteries of light and shall receive them."[12]

No one with the eyes of spiritual understanding opened can doubt that this prophecy is being fulfilled in this present time. Theology, dogma and materialism have alike misinterpreted this supreme judgment of the Christos. The Holy Spirit will test the souls of mankind as by fire, and just as the Kingdom of God cometh not by observation, so also will the purification of the race be so gradual that only when the signs appear in the sun (the male) and in the Moon (the woman), and the Stars (the children) shall *fail*, will those who are *left*" realise the transformation that has taken place in the ones nearest to them, they themselves remaining unchanged.

On each plane of consciousness there is a limit both of time and experience. If the soul has not learnt her lesson in each during the period of her probation, she is as it were shut out, the doors are closed to the higher development. She returns to learn the lesson in a severer form in the next reincarnation, and finds it harder and more difficult because she has clothed herself in the grosser habiliments of matter, added to her matter impure combinations, instead of rendering it finer and more susceptible to the higher vibrations, to which only the pure in heart can

---

[1] See "Pistis Sophia". Mead, pp. 318-19.

respond. And from her is taken even what she appeareth to have gathered, for as dross it has been tried in the fire, and perished in the burning.

The Gnostics taught the true meaning of the "Going Forth out of Egypt," the eternal cosmic process of the soul's progression from the material to the spiritual. All who are slaves to the body are the ignorant and sensual, who crave after the fleshpots of Egypt, the lower nature. To come forth out of Egypt is to leave or control the animal nature, the grosser desires and instincts, and raise them to a higher plane. To pass through the Red Sea is to cross over, to leave behind the ocean of generation with its lust and desire, i.e., the animal and sensual nature, which is hidden in the blood. Yet even then the soul is not safe, for she enters the desert of unfulfilled desire, of doubt, of fear, of apprehension, due to the embryonic condition of the mind, which has not yet assimilated the things that are eternal. The soul is hungry, thirsty and forlorn, and is attacked by the "Gods of Destruction," who seek to destroy those who escape the "Gods of Generation." That is to say, the soul, having ceased to create and produce on the lower plane the things of time, has not yet acquired sufficient spiritual substance to create and bring forth on the higher the things that are eternal. She has crucified her lower self, but the true self has not risen, for she has not crossed the Heavenly Jordan into the Promised Land.

"When," say the Gnostics, "he waters of the Jordan (i.e., of the creative forces) flow downwards, then is the generation of men; but when they flow upward then is the creation of the Gods. Jesus was one who had caused the Waters of Jordan to flow upward."

When Salome asked the Lord how long should death hold sway, He answered, "So long as ye women bring forth; for I came to end the labour of the woman." And Salome said unto Him, "I have then done well in not bringing forth." And the Lord answered and said, "Eat of every pasture, but of that which hath the bitterness of death eat not." And when Salome asked him when shall these things be known, the Lord said, "When ye shall tread upon the vesture of shame, and when the two shall be one, and the male with the female, neither male nor female."

The work, the labour, the travail of the woman will be accomplished, for in generation the matrix is the crucible wherein matter undergoes transmutation, transmission, cleansing, refining, reforming; development and evolution depend upon Maya, "the Great Sea," the Mother of cleansing and purifying. Therefore, when the perfected human is produced the woman shall see of the travail of her soul, and be satisfied. And in the Pleroma "there shall be no more sea," but "the woman" clothed with the sun, and wearing the crown of the seven stars—the perfected divine virtues.

So as to attain this consummation, the vital force of the Eternal Creative Spirit, now expended in generation, and desecrated to self-gratification, will be retained in the system for self-development, for the growth of the true human, the aspiration of all philosophies and of all races of men. "For the feminine is within the masculine. The male has to evolve the woman within him latent but potent." The woman-form is the inner sanctuary which is slowly evolving to the outer, absorbing all things into its own similitude, so that God (the Elohim) may be all in all. The mystics of all time have foreseen this inevitable evolution of mankind, and every religion has foreshadowed it in its symbolic ritual and in its most sacred arcana.[2]

For instance, Iamblichus explains that the emasculation of Attis by the Mother of the Gods "signifies the Power above calling into itself the male energy of the soul." Attis was divested of his lower, earthly part, and then translated to the Upper World. And to this truth not only Rhea, but all creation, beareth testimony; and this is the great and unknown mystery, hidden amongst the Egyptians and yet manifested, for Osiris standeth in the temple before Isis." This supreme mystery could only be divulged to the initiates and to those worthy to receive so momentous a truth. It has been hid from the multitude until the consciousness of the race, as a whole, had sufficiently evolved, physically and psychologically, to be able to respond sympathetically to the higher vibrations of the universal consciousness, and thus intelligently aid in the individual synthesis of the finer particles of matter.

"Treading down the vesture of shame" signifies the rending of the fleshly veil, which has concealed from man his true self. This is being accomplished by science, by research in the natural law governing sex-manifestation, and in the knowledge thus gained being widely disseminated in popular phraseology. Thus mankind will be prepared for the great organic changes that will take place in the human body, of

---

[2] See *The Kabbalah Unveiled: A Book of Beginnings*, by Gerald Massey; *The Rosicrucians, Morgenrothe*, by J. Pulsford. Paracelsus, Jacob Boehme, Lawrence Oliphant, J. Street, and many other mystics teach the same truth.

which there are already many premonitory signs; and "man will himself be capable of recognising and applying this great central truth of sex and its original and ultimate nature." Recognising the divine Womanhood within him, he will keep himself pure, a worthy temple for the Holy Spirit. "Thou wilt save my darling from the lions." "Thou wilt not leave my soul in Hell;" that Hell where the serpent dieth not, and desire is not quenched. "Thou wilt keep him in perfect peace whose soul is stayed on thee."

No sayings of the Christ in the Gospels have been more garbled and misrepresented than those which directly allude to this sublime subject. Take, for instance, the sentences in Matthew: ch. 5, v. 27, 28, "and ye have heard that it was said by them of old time, Thou shalt not commit adultery; but I say unto you. That whosoever looketh on a woman to lust after her hath committed adultery with her already in his heart." Here "woman" includes all women, the virgin and the wife, therefore the adultery spoken of is not of the flesh, but of the spirit. The man is unfaithful to the bride within him—to the subjective "woman-soul" when he desires sensually the objective woman, even though she be a maid or his wife. This was the hard lesson that the disciples could not grasp, and which made them exclaim in despair, "If the case of the man be so with his wife, it is not good to marry." And Christ answers, "all men cannot receive this saying save they to whom it is given," *i.e.*, until the soul has learnt its potential Divinity, and its own latent creative powers, independent of all extraneous and external material factors.

"For," said the Gnostics, "this is the gate of Heaven, and this is the House of God; wherein the Good God dwells alone, into which no impure man shall come, no psychic, no fleshly man, but it is kept under watch for the spiritual alone, where they must come, and, casting away their garments, all become bridegrooms, made virgin by the Virginal Spirit. For such a man is the Virgin with child, who conceives and brings forth a child (*the Divine Life*) which is neither psychic, animal, nor fleshly, but a blessed aeon of aeons." For in each soul is "the indivisible point, which is the primeval spark in the body, and which no man knoweth save only the spiritual," for it is the germ of the Kingdom of Heaven. "Cease to seek after God (as without thee) seek Him from out of thyself . . . thou shalt find Him in thyself, one and many just as the atom, thus finding from thyself a way out of thyself."[3] Having found the Divine in thyself, thou canst expand to the Divine things that Jesus attained (literally gained by working) Godship; " He ate and drank in a peculiar manner, without any waste. The power of continence was so great in Him that his food did not decay in Him, for He Himself was without decay," having no corruption in Him. So writes Valentinus, who probably was a contemporary of the disciples.

Thus the Christ triumphed over the weaker animal power of generation; therefore the God of Generation, one of whose manifestations is Death, had no authority over him. He returned after His sojourn in the grave, with the transfigured or psychic body of the regenerated man, " the first born of the Sons of God;" the same body that was crucified

---

[3] "The tenets of Monoimus."

on the tree, having active in it all its latent potential properties. Being made of the substance of His Mother, the Holy Spirit, it was incorruptible and immortal. The Son of Man (*the lower nature*) was crucified, so that the Son of God might rise and ascend to Heaven.

Here observe how closely the Gnostics are in accord with modern biological science, which conclusively demonstrates that reproduction is another name for death. "Now the impure womb, or sphere of generation, can only produce mortal men, but the virgin, or pure womb, the sphere of light, can produce men, immortal or Gods."

It is the descent of the Perfect Man or Logos (*the Divine Life*) into the pure man that can alone still the birth-pangs of the carnal man.[4] It is the birth of the Christos in the Living Soul, whereby we "show ourselves rulers over the inferior creation within us." This condition is typified by the baptism of cleansing and the garment of white, and the descent of the dove, the Alpha and the Omega, who makes its abode with the soul that has attained to the whole seven spheres of the world-soul (the cosmic life), which are all the elements or powers contained in the Supernal Mother, the Eternal Wisdom, Love, Power, and Holiness. And herein is the great mystery. "The one contains in itself implicitly the three incomprehensibles, Noughtness, Oneness and Naught. Thus the One is the representative of the upper tetrad. And since all numbers

---

[4] Complete individuation, which implies internal and external completeness, not only precludes reproduction, but includes as a preliminary, uniformity of type, which, in the ages to come, will be accomplished in the human race. "Wherefore blessed is the barren that is undefiled. She shall have fruit in the visitation of souls." Wisdom, iii., 13. How crudely foolish and ignorant in the light of these sublime truths are the diatribes of quidnuncs on the decreasing birth rate, the material sign of soul evolution.

come from the One, this tetrad is called the All-Mother, or Wisdom above." And from Her proceeds the Daughter, the lower Wisdom, the World soul, and returns to Her when her travail is accomplished.

Now every divine element, as above said, with all its sub sounds, notes, letters and substances, are contained potentially in the Divine Mother. Thus "the Soul, before she gave herself to body was an auditor of divine harmony, and hence, when she proceeded into body, and heard melodies of such a kind as especially preserve the divine vestige of harmony, she embraced these, from them re-collected divine harmony, and tends and is allied to it, and as much as possible participates of it,"[5] yet because of her incompleteness, the soul cannot name the lost word that upholds all in harmony, nor can she pronounce the name that is above all names, and, as the Gnostics taught, is above that of the Father. For a Name is a definition of properties, and until the soul knows and partakes of the divine qualities she cannot pronounce the ineffable Name.[6]

"And the power of the Christ which descends, is the seed of the Pleroma, containing in itself both the Father and the Son, and the unnamable power of the Silence, the Mother (which is only known through them), now this power of the Silence, this Peace and Comfort, is the Holy Spirit." "Even," as Christ declared, "the Spirit of Truth; whom the world cannot receive, because it seeth Her not, neither knoweth Her." How then could the world name the Supernal Mother of all Truth?

---

[5] *Lamblichus on the Mysteries*, translated by Thomas Taylor, pp. 133-4.

[6] "That name." writes a modern mystic, "seems ever to diffuse itself in the world, but is repelled by so many obstacles that it is forced to return upon itself and withdraw into silence." Louis Claude de Saint Martin.

Therefore sang the Gnostics of the souls that had attained, "They (the blessed ones) have drunk of wine that makes men thirst no more, nor suffer fleshly lust. So with the living spirit they glorify Truth's Father, and sing their praise to Wisdom's Mother." It is here recognised that the Truth must be engendered and brought forth in the masculine phase of consciousness. The Father and the Son must be made perfect in the Truth, for "She is the Strength, Kingdom, Power, and Majesty of all ages."

For "The Maiden" (*the virgin Soul*) "is Light's daughter, in her the King's radiance is treasured. Majestic her look and delightsome; in radiant beauty she shineth. Truth crowneth her head: Joy sports at her feet."

"The King's radiance" is constituted of the conserved transmuted creative energy.

What also can be more beautiful in every spiritual sense than two of the sacramental invocations addressed in hymn form to the Divine Feminine, and of which the mystic meaning is being revealed at the present day?

"Come Thou Holy Name of Christ, Name above all names: (*that is to say, the unspeakable name of the Hidden Mystery, the lost Name of the Universe, that will only be found and uttered when all things attain their consummation*). Come, Power from above; come, Perfect Mercy; come, highest Gift!

"Thou, Mother of Compassion, come: come Spouse of Him, the man; come, thou revealer of the mysteries concealed; thou Mother of the seven mansions, come, who in the eighth hath found thy rest; (*i.e., when the seven phases of consciousness are perfected.*)

"Come, Thou who art more ancient far than the five holy Limbs—Mind, Thought, Reflection, Thinking, Reasoning; commune with those of later birth.

"Come Holy Spirit, purge Thou their reins and heart!"

The second prayer runs thus:

"Come, highest Gift; thou perfect Mercy, come; Thou knower of the Chosen's mysteries, descend; Thou who dost share in all the noble striver's struggles, come!

"Come, Silence, Thou Revealer of the mighty things of all the Greatness; come, thou that dost make manifest, the hidden, and make the secret plain!

"Come, Holy Dove,[7] mother of the two young twins (*Truth and Wisdom*), come hidden Mother, revealed in deeds alone (*i.e., in the fruits of the Spirit.*)

"Come, Thou who givest joy to all who are at one with Thee; come and commune with us in this thanksgiving (Eucharist) which we are making in thy name in this love feast (agape) to which we have assembled at thy call! " And again is this suggestive passage.

"I invoke Thee, O Light, who art above every power of the Father, Thou who art called Light and Spirit and Life; for Thou hast reigned in the body."

---

[7] The Dove is the Alpha and the Omega, and is symbolised in the baptism ceremony by the descent of the Dove upon the initiate who has attained in himself to the whole number of all the elements or powers contained in the World-Mother, the Eternal Wisdom. See *Fragments of a Faith Forgotten.*

"For Thine incorruptible Spirit is in all things,"[8] said, also of old, the Jewish seer.

In the Acts of John, Christ explains to the beloved apostle the mystery of the Cross, and the mystery of the Limbs that shall be gathered from all parts of the universe, when he appears to St. John in a cave on the Mount of Olives, while His earthly body hung upon the Cross on Calvary.

He shows him in a vision a cross of light set up, and about the cross a great multitude, and therein one form and one likeness; and on the cross another multitude not having one form, and I (writes John) saw the Lord Himself above the cross, not having any shape[9] but only a voice; and a voice not such as was familiar to us, but a sweet, kind voice, and one only of God (*the Elohim*) saying unto me: "John, it is needful that one should hear these things from me; for I have need of one who will hear. This cross of light is sometimes called the Word by me for your sakes, sometimes Mind, sometimes Jesus, sometimes Christ, —Door—Way—Bread—Seed—Resurrection—Son—Christ, —Door—Way—Bread—Seed—Resurrection.

"Now these things it is called as towards men, but as to what it is in truth, as conceived of in itself, and as spoken of to thee—it is the marking off (delimitation) of all things, the firm necessity that are fixed, and were settled in the harmony of Wisdom. And whereas it is Wisdom

---

[8] Wisdom of Solomon, xii. 1.

[9] In the Highest there is no form, only Light, and its manifestation in colour, according to the properties of the inherent virtues. Blue is Love. Yellow is Wisdom. Carmine is Creative Energy, Green is Intelligence, Purple is Supremacy and Initiation, Violet is Devotion, Red is Aspiration.

in harmony (or fitly ordered) there are on the Right and Left Powers, Principalities, Sources and Daemons, Energies, Threats, Wrath, Accusers, Satan, and (Below) the lower Root from which hath proceeded the nature of the things in genesis."

This is the Cosmic Cross within the Cosmic Circle. It is the Centre of Eternal Energy, of the creative activities. It is the Cross with the four radii, the eternal Sun-Wheel of the Divinity that shapes the Universe in Love, Wisdom, Power, and Harmony. It is the Divine Spirit and Substance in Cosmic Gestation, whereby, through involution and evolution, all that is past is made new, all that is present is manifest, all that is future is framed. Herein are created the Archetypal Worlds, perfect in the Eternal Ideation, and pronounced "very good." Here are the Spheres of Being and the Vortex of the Elements: here also is the Pleroma or Fulness, the Divine Balance immutable and unchangeable, for the Centre is the perfect Rest.

"This, then." continues the Invisible One, is the cross which fixed all things apart by reason, and marked off the things that come from genesis, the things below it, and then compacted all into one whole."

When the One is divided there may be harmony in the parts, but no completeness in Unity until that which is prefigured is perfected. Only the lost Chord of the Keynote can sound the perfect symphony. But to return to the narrative.

"This is not the cross of wood which thou wilt see when thou hast descended, nor am I He that is upon the cross, whom now thou seest not but only hearest a voice.

"By the others, the many, I have been thought to be what I am not, though I am not what I was. And they will (still) say of me what is base and not worthy of Me.[10]

"Now the multitude of one aspect that is about the cross is the lower nature (*man-in-the-making out of one substance*), and those whom thou seest on the cross, if they have not one form it is because not yet hath every limb of Him who came down been gathered together (*i.e., man in the phases of individuated consciousness*). But when the upper nature shall be taken up and the race which is repairing to me, in obedience to my voice, then that which (as yet) hears me not, shall become as thou art, and shall no longer be what it is now, but above them (of the lower world) even as I am now.

"For so long as thou callest not thyself mine, I am not what I am (*i.e., my limbs are scattered*). But if hearing thou hearkenest unto me, then shalt thou be as I am, and I shall be what I was, when I have thee as I am with myself. For from this (centre) thou art.

"Nothing, therefore, of the things which they will say of Me have I suffered. For what I am that I alone know, and none else. Suffer me then to keep that which is my own, and that which is thine behold thou through me, and behold me in truth that I am, not what I said, but what thou art able to know, for thou art kin to me.

---

[10] Truly has the Mother been despised and rejected of men, truly she has trod the winepress alone, and of her sons there were none with her. She has borne in truth the offscourings of all things. According to the old Chaldean oracle, "the wild beasts of the earth shall inhabit thy vessel." The Shekinah shall be hidden behind the veil. Her Sanctuary shall be trodden down.

"Thou hearest that I suffered, yet I suffered not: that I suffered not yet did I suffer; that I was pierced. Yet was I not smitten, that I was hanged, yet was I not hanged; that blood flowed from me, yet it flowed not. In a word, those things that they say of me I had not, and the things that they say not, those I suffered. Now what they are I will shadow forth (riddle) for thee, for I know that thou wilt understand.

"See thou therefore in Me the slaying of a Word (Logos) the piercing of a Word, the blood of a Word, the wounding of a Word, the hanging of a Word, the passion of a Nord, the nailing (fixing or joining) of a Word, the death of a Word. And by a Word I mean Man. First, then, understand the Word, then shalt thou understand the Lord, and thirdly, the Man, and what is his Passion."[11]

For "the Word was made flesh and dwelt among us." And lo! no man knoweth it, nor can utter it till be has grown to the similitude of the One whose Name it is. Therefore Man as now constituted is not the Word, but the Word is forming in him, and the true Humanity is evolving through the manifestation of the Divine Feminine in the human Soul. This is the spiritual birth of Mary, the Virgin, who brings forth the immortal offspring in the shadow of Death and in the Valley of Humiliation.

No words, then, can be plainer to the spiritual sense that these remarkable sentences from the Great Silence, during the crucifixion of the Christ, the Manifestation of the Divine Feminine in the apotheosis of the Male Element. The Cosmic Cross is, as it were, the Body of

---

[11] See *Fragments of a Faith Forgotten*. Mead, pp.

the Divine Mother, the eternal substance, wherein, through all transitory transformations and transmutations. She is ever crucified afresh, wherein all the members of the universe are written, being yet imperfect, in which the Supreme travail of Creation is accomplished with the groan and the cry and the great tribulation, with a sorrow that cannot be uttered, too deep for words, too awful for expression. This is the Lamb slain from the foundation of the World, by whose blood the nations are healed. Thus the Divine Mother in her diremption as Man—the universe, the Becoming—is crucified in Space, that is to say, limited by necessity, change and death. "Is there any sorrow like unto my sorrow? Is it naught to you, all ye that pass by?"

But when *Man* (the objective manifestation) assumes his true nature, made perfect through suffering, he is at one with the Divine Feminine, in whom all things abide. Then the harmony of Wisdom is established,[12] and "Wisdom is justified in all her children" gathered, as units, from all quarters of the Cosmos, and the many become the One, made after one likeness, both below and above. For under all name is She called, yet all these names are combined in One; all lights proceed from one light, and the Cross of limitation becomes the boundless circle of infinite glory.[13]

---

[12] Wisdom hath built her house, she hath hewn out her seven pillars." Pro. IX. 1. The pillars are the seven psychic spheres of soul evolution, in which the soul is perfected.

[13] In all the archaic faiths, the symbolism of the Cross as the emblem of Blessing is always associated with a female Divinity. It is represented in the spotless lotus flower, self -procreative, and in the sacred rose bearing in the centre the cruciform symbol that typified the abode of the Gods. The archaic Venus, the self-existent One, the immaculate Virgin, was depicted as bringing her Cross of Glory from Heaven, so that all things on earth might be formed in Love and Purity. Her Symbol was also the

The Christos, the Divine Life, the word formed in Substance, crucified in the beginning, becomes one with that which He truly is, the Name, Power and Majesty of the invisible Divine Mother. Thus the source of the Cross is the Man whom no man can comprehend. He is the Father, who is hid in the Mother, "The 'Workman," the Anointed or Appointed of God, who goeth forth to work the works of God, and to bring them to immutable perfection. It is the God in Man that suffers the Divine Incompleteness.

Therefore Jesus saith: "Blessed is the man who crucifieth the world and doth not let the world crucify him." And when asked by the disciples what is the life and will of the Father, Jesus answers "that the *Life of His Father* consists in their purifying their souls from all earthly stain and making them to become the Race of Mind (*self-luminous and self-knowing*), so that they may he filled with understanding, and by His teaching perfect themselves, and be saved from the rulers of this World and its endless snares." "For," saith Jesus, "Blessed is the man who knoweth this Word (*the Logos, the Divine Life*), and hath brought down the heaven, and borne the Earth and raised it heavenwards; and it (the Earth) becometh the midst, for it is a nothing.' "

The natural law of our spiritual progress is our renunciation of and disentanglement from the lower sense life. Not a living out of the World, but living in it, but not of it. The Soul makes the great and eternal choice.

Wheel of Light and Life—the four radii of the cosmic cross. Among the Assyrians, Phoenicians, Persians, Indians, and the races of Asia. Minor, the cross as a feminine symbol was the type of the tree of life and immortality. As the symbol of the curse, it is always associated with a male victim.

The Soul is, as it were, suspended in space and time, in the midst of spiritual, intellectual, and material phenomena. Amidst the diversity, division, and dispersion, she has to seek the One element, the One law, and the One Divinity, and in the Unity to find the lost Word and the Great Name. And it shall be her new Name by which she shall be called.

And thus it will be that the mystery that is from the beginning will be completed. The fashion of this world passeth away, and behold all things become new unto the soul that entereth the light of lights.[14]

"I am thou," says the Divine Mother, "and thou art I, the I on, and wheresoever thou art I am there, and I am sown (or scattered) in all; from whencesoever thou wiliest, thou gatherest me, and gathering me thou gatherest thyself."

And the perfected Soul makes answer: —

"I have recognised myself and gathered myself together from all sides. I have sown no children to the Ruler (*the Lord of this world*), but have torn up his roots (*of lust and sensuality*). I have gathered together my limbs that were scattered abroad, and I know Thee who Thou art."

To sum up; from this superficial and cursory glance at the Gnostic philosophy, we may gather that it possessed a clear insight of the cosmic law of infinite progression. Shorn of many crude hypotheses and grotesque symbology, clothed in the anthropomorphic phraseology universally connected in all ages with spiritual truths, the mysticism of the Gnostics approached

---

[14] The Chaldean Oracle says. "Things divine cannot be obtained by those whose intellectual eye is directed to body; but those only can arrive at the possession of them who, stripped of their garments, hasten to the Summit."—*The Mystical Hymns of Orpheus*. Translated by Thomas Taylor. p. 193.

the elucidation of many abstruse problems, and intuitively divined the sequence of natural laws in the spiritual world, of which the working is only now being revealed by the arduous researches of science and the higher consciousness of the Soul. We may in part realise how high was the ideal of life set before the initiates to the sacred mysteries. With the Gnostics there was in the abstract no "fallen man," but an ascending humanity, a humanity that would transcend man himself, when he recognised where he had disobeyed and deviated from the natural Law of order and harmony. They knew that the soul must be built up, clothed upon, grow, as in natural evolution, to her full stature of righteousness, joy and peace in the spirit.

Each individual must choose the good and refuse the evil. There was no salvation except through the redemption of the soul. The Gnostics insisted that the foundation of the Christian life was character, not ritual; practice, not theology; principle, not dogma, the Spirit working in the flesh, not the Spirit working independent of the flesh. They did not minimise the cost of the soul's conflict; they fully recognised the necessity of the rod and spur of self-discipline. But they opined that no soul can be disobedient to the heavenly vision, when beyond the surrounding shadows it catches a faint glimpse of the Reality. It is impelled forward by the very force and magnitude of its inner-consciousness, by the glory that is revealed to it. To that awakened soul return is impossible, even to bury its dead; the stricken Gods of the past, the Heart's best beloved, the revered Father of its Thought, and the Son of its own making. All pass, as it soars into the Infinite, where there is neither shape, nor form, nor speech, nor language, nor any simultitude of the things of Space and Time.

PLATE 4

The Soul in adoration of the Divine in the High Heaven of Purity.

In this figure is symbolised the achievement, the attainment, the fulfilment of the Soul's travail. In the first place, note the colour. In the original drawing, the blue is of the purest cobalt. Blue is the colour of Love. God is Love. Occultists state that it is the last colour to be beheld and known in the world of sense. The human eye has not yet seen it nor comprehended it in its intensity. For no mortal has seen God at any time, nor has the mind of man fathomed the Divine Love, nor formed a conception of its infinite Holiness. But the Soul in her apotheosis is clothed in the Divine Love, and in the Righteousness of the Christos, the Divine Life. She has entered into the Oneness. She is in the Supreme Radiance of the White Light of Purity. For mark there is no coloured background, the Wings of Love soar in the Light of Lights, from which all light, colour, sound, and form proceed.

Secondly, note the form. The Soul has evolved to the similitude of the Lily, the symbol of the Immaculate Virgin of Inherent Holiness. In the drawing, the grand sweep of the petals is curtailed by the size of the paper, but the lines are magnificent in their strength and unfaltering purpose. For Love perfected is omnipotent and omniscient, self-existent, and self-creative. The Soul has risen with the wings of the Dove, emblematical of the Holy Spirit, by whose attributes alone can the Soul achieve the Highest.

Thus, after this world's fitful fevers, after the struggle, the conflict, and the pain, the Soul has found the Peace that passeth understanding. She has awakened to the Divine Likeness, and is satisfied with it.

THE ALLEGORY OF THE WORLD'S SOUL

"The bread of understanding shall she feed him with, and give him the water of Wisdom to drink."—Eccl. XV. 3.

"The Soul of the World flew lightly
Over the sun-loving Earth;
She hovered o'er every flower,
Softly kissed all Life to birth.

She knew that she held within her
In some mysterious form,
The powers of the Hereafter
Both the sunshine and the storm.

That, unshackled, free, benignant,
She could bless the teeming world;
Her's were Love's conquering army
And banners of God unfurled.

She gazed with clear eye and vision
On the evolving great To-be,
When out of the Now imperfect
The Perfect man yet should see.

Out of finite, small beginnings
Should the mighty Whole up-grow;
The Fatherhood and Motherhood,
From the seed the race should sow.

The triumphs of the intellect
Potent victories of mind,
The slow but sure development
Of the best in human kind.

And she cried, with eyes all smiling,
As men worshipped at her feet,
"Behold me! I am thy lode-star
The life of all hearts that beat.

"I come as the embodiment
Of the Love that is divine:
Of the Love that fills all Heaven
Shall my true love be the sign.

"I will be myself the guerdon
Of each brave and noble deed;
I will give the inspiration
To each toiler in his need.

"To me ye may come in sorrow,
To me may ye come in pain;
And my presence is the token
That God's righteousness shall reign."

The wondering World lay silent,
It could neither do nor dare;
But it sheltered in its bosom
Heaven's angel unaware.

The Soul of the World lay sobbing,
Chained down to the cold damp earth:
Long had the sunshine departed,
Hush'd in gloom the songs of mirth.

The chains were fast on her ankles,
The fetters bound on her wrist;
"I came to you, oh ye people!
And ye have done what ye list.

"I came with the gift of healing,
  Blessing all and being blessed,
I came as the guide of Heaven
  Towards the eternal quest.

"My hands were full of earth's roses;
  On my pure lips were the pearls;
In my heart the infinite charity
  That enfolds the rolling worlds.

"I would have given you wisdom,
  And bread from the source of life;
The fruits of peace would have fed you,
  Instead of the spoils of strife.

"But ye bound, and beat, and bled me,
  And ye kept me cramp's, confin'd;
The words that would save the nations
  Are lost in the winter wind.

"The earth hath foregone her beauty.
  Her youth and her sense of Spring,
For the Soul, that soared above it,
  Fell wounded with crippled wing.

"The shaft of that brute-like archer
Alas! pierced not me alone;
Take ye the free from the captive?
Form ye a child from a stone?

"My children dreamt of were holy,
Were pure as the summer light.
Are these—say are these, thine or mine,
Dark offspring of blackest Night?

"They came: I could only love them:
My hands and my feet were bound.
I—who could gently have led them
The fair paths of wisdom round.

"I—who was given the beacon
Of the Light that is to be,
Held it high, until they quenched it,
For, blinded, they could not see.

"And I, as I lie here moaning,
Can hear the cries of despair;
The shout and the brawl and the curse
With misery fill the air.

"I deemed the world full of beauty,
A world growing wondrous fair,
With laughter and joy of children
And happiness ev'rywhere.

"They say it is I who hast marr'd it:
I, who hast fallen so low.
God! from whose Heaven I earnest—
Say then, is it I or Thou

"Thou said'st, From the Love eternal
All blessings of good shall grow.
Was the ground, then, fallow for evil?
Shall they not reap what they sow?

"See. I lie stricken and bleeding:
I hold my life in my hand:
Take it! perchance its sacrifice
May yet purify the land."

There came a sound of murmuring,
The tread of a mighty host;
The voices of men and women;
The sick, the sad, and the lost.

They knelt by the Soul that lay dying,
Bound up her festering sore,
They unclasped her galling fetters,
Made her free for evermore.

They clothed her in gold and purple,
They crowned her with crown of stars;
They strove, in their deep contrition,
To cover the tell-tale scars.

They prayed she should rule and sway them;
Then again the World's Soul smiled;
For in loving arms unfettered
She nestled her own fair child.

Paperbacks also available from
White Crow Books

Elsa Barker—*Letters from
a Living Dead Man*
ISBN 978-1-907355-83-7

Elsa Barker—*War Letters from
the Living Dead Man*
ISBN 978-1-907355-85-1

Elsa Barker—*Last Letters from
the Living Dead Man*
ISBN 978-1-907355-87-5

Richard Maurice Bucke—
Cosmic Consciousness
ISBN 978-1-907355-10-3

Arthur Conan Doyle—
The Edge of the Unknown
ISBN 978-1-907355-14-1

Arthur Conan Doyle—
The New Revelation
ISBN 978-1-907355-12-7

Arthur Conan Doyle—
The Vital Message
ISBN 978-1-907355-13-4

Arthur Conan Doyle with
Simon Parke—*Conversations
with Arthur Conan Doyle*
ISBN 978-1-907355-80-6

Meister Eckhart with Simon Parke—
Conversations with Meister Eckhart
ISBN 978-1-907355-18-9

D. D. Home—*Incidents in my Life Part 1*
ISBN 978-1-907355-15-8

Mme. Dunglas Home; edited,
with an Introduction, by Sir
Arthur Conan Doyle—*D. D.
Home: His Life and Mission*
ISBN 978-1-907355-16-5

Edward C. Randall—
Frontiers of the Afterlife
ISBN 978-1-907355-30-1

Rebecca Ruter Springer—
Intra Muros: My Dream of Heaven
ISBN 978-1-907355-11-0

Leo Tolstoy, edited by Simon
Parke—*Forbidden Words*
ISBN 978-1-907355-00-4

Leo Tolstoy—*A Confession*
ISBN 978-1-907355-24-0

Leo Tolstoy—*The Gospel in Brief*
ISBN 978-1-907355-22-6

Leo Tolstoy—*The Kingdom
of God is Within You*
ISBN 978-1-907355-27-1

Leo Tolstoy—*My Religion:
What I Believe*
ISBN 978-1-907355-23-3

Leo Tolstoy—*On Life*
ISBN 978-1-907355-91-2

Leo Tolstoy—*Twenty-three Tales*
ISBN 978-1-907355-29-5

Leo Tolstoy—*What is Religion
and other writings*
ISBN 978-1-907355-28-8

Leo Tolstoy—*Work While
Ye Have the Light*
ISBN 978-1-907355-26-4

Leo Tolstoy—*The Death of Ivan Ilyich*
ISBN 978-1-907661-10-5

Leo Tolstoy—*Resurrection*
ISBN 978-1-907661-09-9

Leo Tolstoy with Simon Parke—
Conversations with Tolstoy
ISBN 978-1-907355-25-7

Howard Williams with an Introduction
by Leo Tolstoy—*The Ethics of Diet:
An Anthology of Vegetarian Thought*
ISBN 978-1-907355-21-9

Vincent Van Gogh with Simon Parke—
Conversations with Van Gogh
ISBN 978-1-907355-95-0

Wolfgang Amadeus Mozart with Simon
Parke—*Conversations with Mozart*
ISBN 978-1-907661-38-9

Jesus of Nazareth with Simon Parke—
Conversations with Jesus of Nazareth
ISBN 978-1-907661-41-9

Thomas à Kempis with Simon
Parke—*The Imitation of Christ*
ISBN 978-1-907661-58-7

Julian of Norwich with Simon
Parke—*Revelations of Divine Love*
ISBN 978-1-907661-88-4

Allan Kardec—*The Spirits Book*
ISBN 978-1-907355-98-1

Allan Kardec—*The Book on Mediums*
ISBN 978-1-907661-75-4

Emanuel Swedenborg—*Heaven and Hell*
ISBN 978-1-907661-55-6

P.D. Ouspensky—*Tertium Organum:
The Third Canon of Thought*
ISBN 978-1-907661-47-1

Dwight Goddard—*A Buddhist Bible*
ISBN 978-1-907661-44-0

Michael Tymn—*The Afterlife Revealed*
ISBN 978-1-970661-90-7

Michael Tymn—*Transcending the
Titanic: Beyond Death's Door*
ISBN 978-1-908733-02-3

Guy L. Playfair—*If This Be Magic*
ISBN 978-1-907661-84-6

Guy L. Playfair—*The Flying Cow*
ISBN 978-1-907661-94-5

Guy L. Playfair —*This House is Haunted*
ISBN 978-1-907661-78-5

Carl Wickland, M.D.—
Thirty Years Among the Dead
ISBN 978-1-907661-72-3

John E. Mack—*Passport to the Cosmos*
ISBN 978-1-907661-81-5

Peter & Elizabeth Fenwick—
The Truth in the Light
ISBN 978-1-908733-08-5

Erlendur Haraldsson—
Modern Miracles
ISBN 978-1-908733-25-2

Erlendur Haraldsson—
At the Hour of Death
ISBN 978-1-908733-27-6

Erlendur Haraldsson—
The Departed Among the Living
ISBN 978-1-908733-29-0

Brian Inglis—*Science and Parascience*
ISBN 978-1-908733-18-4

Brian Inglis—*Natural and Supernatural:
A History of the Paranormal*
ISBN 978-1-908733-20-7

Ernest Holmes—*The Science of Mind*
ISBN 978-1-908733-10-8

Victor & Wendy Zammit —*A Lawyer
Presents the Evidence For the Afterlife*
ISBN 978-1-908733-22-1

Casper S. Yost—*Patience
Worth: A Psychic Mystery*
ISBN 978-1-908733-06-1

William Usborne Moore—
Glimpses of the Next State
ISBN 978-1-907661-01-3

William Usborne Moore—
The Voices
ISBN 978-1-908733-04-7

John W. White—
The Highest State of Consciousness
ISBN 978-1-908733-31-3

Stafford Betty—
The Imprisoned Splendor
ISBN 978-1-907661-98-3

Paul Pearsall, Ph.D. —
Super Joy
ISBN 978-1-908733-16-0

All titles available as eBooks, and selected titles available in Hardback and Audiobook formats from www.whitecrowbooks.com